Moments Of Clarity

Discover the essence of your true self

Nelo Phiri

BookLeaf Publishing

India | USA | UK

Made with ❤ on the BookLeaf Publishing Platform

www.bookleafpub.in

www.bookleafpub.com

Dedication

To my belief in the power of God,
for every moment of doubt
conquered,
For every scar worn as a badge of
resilience,
For every humble moment that
gave ode to my ancestors,
For believing in the beauty of
becoming,
And for trusting the process of
healing and growth.
To God,
For being the steady hand that
uplifts me,

The light that pierced every
shadow,
The love that never wavered,
And the source of every word
poured from my soul.
With deepest gratitude and love
to all.

Preface

This collection is a journey, one of self-discovery, healing, and the divine connection between the human spirit and God's grace. Each word represents a moment of clarity, triumph, vulnerability, and faith.

In writing these poems, I found strength in embracing my imperfections and celebrating my victories. I discovered that the greatest act of love is first offered to oneself and that surrendering

to God's plan is a source of
endless peace.

These pages are not just poetry,
they are prayers, reflections, and
reminders of how far I have
come. They are meant to inspire,
to uplift, and to encourage
anyone walking their own path
to know they are never truly
alone.

May every word echo with hope,
resilience, and faith. And may
this book serve as a testament to

the beauty of a life surrendered
to love.

Acknowledgements

With a heart full of gratitude, I offer thanks to those who have walked alongside me on this journey.

To God, my ever-present guide, for lighting my path even in my darkest moments. Your grace and love have been the foundation of every step I've taken and every spoken word I've written.

To my family and friends, thank you for your grace, love, and encouragement. You have lifted me when I couldn't stand on my own, and celebrated with me when I soared.

To the moments of struggle and triumph, both have shaped me. The challenges taught me resilience, and the victories taught me gratitude.

And finally, to every reader, thank you for holding this book in your hands and allowing these words to touch your heart and inspire your mind. May every word bring insight to love, and inspiration to your journey of self discovery.

With deepest love and

appreciation,
Nelo Phiri

I. Moment of Clarity, part I

'Honey, I am a grown Woman.'
Glowing and flowing in a more
positive direction.
Moving and grooving according
to what moves me, I continue a
weekly routine that is in
congruence with who I am and
have always been. Loving,
peaceful, and growing.
consistent on my wellness and
vision for a better future is my
foundation. Rooted in prioritizing

self care. Care. Care about the energy we give, care about our experience here. I love it here. Personally, I'm excited about my life, living in my purpose with the intention to enjoy it. Professionally, I'm a working progress. Working and progressing in my time management and organizing my daily bread.

Money is not the motive, moving in abundance is. Money certainly helps measure tangible value, acquire assets, and can be a family's daily bread.

I don't ask for money, I work for
it.
I am the woman that not only
has money but is financially
savvy. Effectively and efficiently
managing money for myself and
others.
I am the woman that balances 3
businesses and a family of 4,
including myself.
I am the woman that is timely,
but also knows when to move on
time.
Life is to be embraced, so laugh
and celebrate the past and enjoy
everyday like it's the last.

I love to live, because I live to love. I live to love, because I am Ms. Love.

II. My Forever Love

There will be a day,
Where I will find my love,
my heart will stop breaking,
& I'll live without ever faking.
On my way up, I will not regret a
thing,
I will simply say thank you,for a
promising love that comes with a
ring.
Today I will pray,

that God brings me through the days, where I build up, and won't be held astray.

He is my forever love, one that I'll love forever. Because it is so simple, I can not complain, we are whole even without each other, but we still remain .

Because I am your person and you're my forever love, I pray we stand together, led by the good Lord above.

III. Moment of Clarity, part II

What am I clear about in this moment?
I am clear about all I am.
I am the seeds that were planted in me.
I am the people that stood by me.
I am the person that I am, forever.
For forever, I lean into who I am.
Love.

Working to be in alignment with
my Heavenly Father.
So Patient. So Kind. And never
fails.
Developing and growing my
Balance, balancing my calm and
exciting personality.
Focus, focusing on keeping my
eyes on the prize.
and *Footwork*, moving with ease,
to the beat of my own drums.
I love it here.
Clear about who I am and where
I'm coming from.
No, not where I was born, but
what I am rooted in.

Though I am a proud African, I resemble most with the human kind.

Abantu, abantu bonse basuma.

I don't know everything, but I am certain, of Jah, Yahweh, Ba Lesa. God. Love.

Without a doubt. Without fear.

I ...remain... Clear.

IV. Tap In

"Tap Innn."

He tells me, of course,

Because I'm married to the

source.

Despite the current circumstance,

it kind of makes me smile, that

day in and day out, I get to speak

to the divine.

Sometimes naughty and not so

nice, but he sure keeps me in

line. Fine, I say, show me the

way.

The way I can glow and flow in a
more positive direction.
Or is it left solely to
interpretation...?
Mmm no, so ladies and
gentlemen, I'm not really here to
say a poem, I'm here so you can
get to know him.
Him; Jah, Ba Lesa , God, Love.
The One from above.
Without a doubt, without fear, I
remain clear.
"So Tap Innn,"
He says.
"In what?" I say. While waiting
for an answer, he stops and

stares. I stare back, knowing that
I know, that he knows, that I
know.
I couldn't help it, a moment of
conversation, for interpretation ,
some things are just not worth
the investigation. Simply
appreciation, for what's already
in front of us.
So tap in, it's a must.

V. I Do This

I do this. What is this?

A form of expression, of my

intention.

My motivation for creative

organization.

One moment at a time, I manifest

good creation.

Clear and obvious to the eye and

mind.

Love is the core of my vibration.

Combating temptation with

positive inspiration.

I love it here.
Rooted in reading, running, and
much needed meditation.
For the purpose of
concentration.
For the interest of effective
conversation.
and good communication.
I share valuable information.
Cash App, $NeloLoves ,
and interviews; life
investigation.
Instagram, Nelo_Loves.
I'll consider your application,
After serious evaluation, or large
compensation.

Much appreciation.

Ms. Love

VI. In Love

I want to be in love,
with someone other than me,
an intimate love,
Can't you see?
Being in love has to be,
double the beauty.
Having love to give
is the best way to Live.
My Mother taught me Love,
The kind of Love that comes from
above.

My God is protective, so I'm
selective.
Communicate, rather than
fornicate.
Longing for the day, where I can
say,
I do.
Because he's not only a fan,
that's my Man.

VII. Dear Men

Dear Men,

Who are you? Because
sometimes, what I believe to be
true, isn't always what you show
me.

Truth is, you are magnificent.
Magical in all ways. Creators of
homes, bridges, and
infrastructure that facilitate our
well-being and our pleasures.
Men, who are you?

Truth is, just as you build
homes,
without a solid foundation, you
can tear them down too.
But ever so patient, ever so kind,
Men, you're the creators of our
world,
Just maintain the right mind.
I love it here.
Actively learning your gentle
ways, so we can embrace your
softness, as much as we embrace
your fortitude.
Men, who are you?
Because if what I believe to be
true, is in fact, a fact.

Men, show me.

VIII. Dear Good People

I love you. I love your style. I
love your being.
You're absolutely contagious.
The life we live is peaceful,
though courageous.
Pleasantly contesting.
Ever so heavenly. Not pushing
the extremity.
Encouraging masculine and
femininity.
Raising humanity.
Higher standards.

We stand for Love.
Good grace, from above.
Oh good people,
You are Loved.

IX. Dear All

Dear All,

I love you. Though deeply rooted in agony, I am free from calamity.

I rest in 10 standards.

Higher standards.

Standards, a form of a word standard.

Something considered by a general consent or agreement.

Standard;

Serving as a basis of measure,

value, or judgment.

for me

higher standards require

gratitude for being here.

One,

Know yourself

Two,

Love yourself

Three,

Prepare Yourself

Four,

Understand Yourself

Five,

Work on Yourself

Six,

Learn Others
Seven,
Love Others
Eight,
Prepare Others
Nine,
Understand Others
Ten,
Work on each Other.
Thank you.

X. What is Love? Part I

Powerful and mighty.

Infinite and lasting.

Generous and pure.

Pure as the wave that clashes on the sand, works its way to your toes and returns back to its ocean.

Generous as the sun that brightens an entire world from sunrise to sunset.

Lasting forever, forever lasting.

Mighty as the universe that's as
powerful as its galaxy, bound
together by gravity.
Just ask yourself, am I nature's
gift to them?

XI. Who is my Son?

Who is my Son? My Son is Yesu.
A peaceful Man. One that is
silently competitive and knows
when to exude his natural
competitive nature. My Son is
athletic. A quick learner and
maintains a brave spirit. One that
learns from mistakes and is
curious about improvement. My
Son enjoys reading stories that
inspire his creativity. Stories that
move him to create something

purposeful. He is observant, enough to discern what's for him and not for him. My Son communicates with me in moments he needs advice or simply wants to talk. He communicates well due to his ability to express himself with self awareness and understanding of his emotions. An emotional intelligence that's in congruence with his IQ. My Son knows when to be social with others, others that appreciate his intellectual conversation and not just his looks, because he is very handsome. When girls like him or when he likes a girl, he will talk to me and his Father to better understand how to approach the situation. My Son is focused on purposeful relationships and experiences with family and progressing in his creativity, academics, working with teammates in his sport, tech, chess club, and other activities that bring out the best in him. My Son loves to be involved with activities that move him and looks forward to knowing Mama and Papa are in the stands supporting proudly. My son knows he does everything for a good purpose. To create a good life for himself and others. So he respects his parents, keeps his eyes on God and maintains his peace.

My Son knows he is loved beyond his parents, because he has a village that loves him. But he also knows he's loved, by God.

XII. Gratitude is the Attitude

I am grateful for the sunrise,

raising my eyes for a new day.

I am grateful for the birds,

singing sweet songs of melodies

that blow me away.

I am grateful for my bed, making

it every morning before saying

my daily bread.

I am grateful for a good word.

Encouraging, inspiring, and

feeding the soul.

I am grateful for breakfast, apples
and oatmeal in a bowl.
I am grateful for a glass of water
that hydrates my body, cleansing
me with purity and good health
to add on to my wealth.
I am grateful for the work I get to
do. Serving God through daily
tasks is the new cool.
I am grateful for goal-setting,
achieving one thing at a time and
sometimes overachieving.
I am grateful I am blossoming,
the best version of me is the
journey.

I am grateful for the gospel,
keeping me humble and faithful
as I see the best in me.
I am grateful for the abundance
that is coming my way, filling me
with goodness, every single day.

XIII. More Coffee, Please

Motherhood is drinking a whole mug of coffee and still feeling drowsy. Where prepping for an extra hour of energy becomes a belly full of useless caffeine, extra sugar and cream also known as imitation cappuccino. Slowly gulped down for an enjoyable impact that you'd hope can get the job done.

It's the moment you think you
can check off your to-do list
while the baby sleeps but also
remember to consider the wise
advice to rest while the baby
sleeps.
Motherhood is exhaustion in
motion.
Moving gracefully, with a smile
on your face; a mix of feeling
blessed and stressed but carrying
it with grace.
More Coffee please, with an extra
shot of espresso, make that to go,
because every moment I'm up is
a moment to make moves.

Motherhood is the knowing that as your child grows, you must grow too. So more coffee please, because though my self care routine requires sleep, my vision is woke, it's expensive, it's luxurious, my vision is to sleep sweet, because Motherhood is sweet.

XIV. I Am Every Woman

I am every Woman,

Carefully created to create, called

to nurture, and embody Love.

To Illuminate the one above.

I am every Woman,

Carefully created to create, called

to nurture, and carry forward the

core of what is the human kind.

Love.

Nothing more, nothing less.

Provide us with peace, deliver us

from stress.

Always having to clean up the
mess, or need to impress.
Discard the worldly images of a
Woman.
Don't be distracted by the diluted
version of who I am, when who I
am is carefully created to create,
the human kind.

*So please, allow me to
reintroduce myself...
My name is G.O.to the Godly.
I am divine, in line with the holy.
Spirit, so please don't control
me.*

Aware, I will not compare.
Equality is simply a formality of
worldly insanity.

This is not a competition, it's a
worldly transition.
A paradigm shift, for clear
recognition.
A moment of silence
As we all recognize the value of a
woman,
With an inhale, take in the
value.

With an exhale, release the
traumas.

So Enough, believing lies about
us.
Enough, shaming our mistakes.
Enough, creating division
amongst us.
Enough, beating on our souls.
Enough, sexually assaulting.
Enough, targeting our
weaknesses for your fear, ego or
your pain.
Be Aware of your greatness, and
simply stay in your lane.

Don't make us go insane.

Grow the individual mind, body,
and spirit.
Fearless.
We need one another.
So Commit to loving yourself,
commit to being kind to
yourself,
and by maintaining the right
mind, we will uplift the human
kind.

I am every Woman,

Carefully created to create, called

to nurture, and embody Love.

To Illuminate the one above.

Cause I ..am .. Ms Love.

XV. I Am That Woman

I Am That, Woman.

Not here to convince you, just

simply admitting to, the facts.

Evolving as we speak.

Speaking of moments to brighten

the paths

Of future generations, such a

sensation.

I Am That Woman.

Heavenly sent, never bent, In

God, I'm content, because he got

me, so no need to vent.

I Am That woman.
Aiming for more, forget the
allure, straight shoota,
Bulls eye when I open my eyes,
on God,
You shoulda pursued her.
I Am That Woman.
Conveying a message of Love,
Spoken words sent from above.
Igniting the passion in orderly
fashion.
I AM That Woman.
Loving out Loud,
Dark, African, and Proud,
A virtuous woman,
No competition,

Proverbs 31 Woman,
The exclusive edition,
Because I Am That Woman.

XVI. Have You Ever?

Have you ever reached a point where you no longer feel comfortable with being vulnerable?

Have you ever come close enough to loving someone that you thought could be "the one."

Have you ever watched someone beat you down emotionally, subconsciously showing you narcissistic energy?

Enough to have you encounter
mental insecurities that make
you question your whole being.
Have you ever stayed up late
using coping mechanisms that
alleviate the pain,
That becomes a crutch to
tolerating life in vain.
Have you ever had so much to
say but say so little because you
don't feel heard.
Have you ever decided to resort
to violence, instead you take
A moment of silence to calm the
worries of the mind, just to find

that only God can save her, so

she puts pen to paper.

Have you ever completed a poem

that puts a smile on your face,

giving you a taste of God's good

grace?

Have you ever simply said thank

you, for all that's made you who

you are? Because what you have

done has made you a star.

XVII. Love At First Sight

I Loved him at first sight,
Never needed to fight,
Just pure delight,
In the way he walked,
In the way he talked.
The motive was intentional,
To be exceptional,
Free from drama,
Blessings from my Mama,
It was love at first sight,
Until we started to fight,
I decided to take flight,

When he talked, I walked away,
Couldn't stand it when he would
play,
With my heart,
A love I never meant to start.
It was Love at first sight.
But now my heart, I choose to
protect,
Never neglect, remembering my
worth is the main intent.
It was Love at first sight, when I
finally saw my own light.

XVIII. Black Beyond Measure

Ain't it funny how...
Actually not funny at all.
At times,
We may use humor and laughter
to cope with our anger,
Using laughter as a mechanism
to tame the danger,
SNL laughing at our pain is
insane,
Comedy Central reporting us to
be the funniest race,

Cool, but ain't it a disgrace,
Knowing all that we've faced.
Let freedom come, when we
decide to abide by the beauty of
our cultures,
dismissing the vultures.
But ain't it funny how, actually
not funny at all.
We don't have to succumb to
stereotypes,
We don't have to internalize the
lies,
We don't have to accept what's
handed to us,
We don't have to entertain or
disguise,

Who we really are..
We are the people of all kinds,
We are the ones enriching the
minds,
of the next generation,
isn't it a sensation,
to know that we are the source of
liberation.
Liberation from oppression and
unsolved mysteries,
to now become healed , appealed,
and concealed.
A gift only found within. Where
do I begin?
Rooted in love, but diluted by sin.

Ain't it funny how...Actually not
funny at all.
A blessing and a curse, like a
white woman clutching her
purse when a brotha walks by,
why?
The Fear of something it could
never find,
That demon in her mind, rooted
from an evil kind.
Black beyond measure, we are
truly a treasure,
spiritually connected, our roots,
intersected,
Attempted to divide us,

but our foundation was
perfected.
Ain't it funny how...
Actually not funny at all.
Either feared or respected.
Black beyond measure,
we are truly a treasure.

XIX. Today

Today, is the day,
where I no longer play, or say,
such things that move me astray,
Today, is the day, where I no
longer fear, cause my dear,
the day is here.
Today is the day, I get to hear,
that our time is near.
So no fear, do I make myself
clear?
A moment of clarity,
Will exercise brevity.

Keeping it short and sweet,
What is for me, is for me,
So lets take a seat.
Enjoying the presence of the
God,
While I slowly nod,
knowing that what's for me, is
for me,
cause my dear, the day is here,
so no fear,
do I make myself clear?

XX. Spoken Word Poet

Honey, I do my part,
I show up for my art.
Beautiful, wavy, and smart,
Baby, I knew that from the start.

I am a Spoken word poet,
I was before I knew it.
Pen to paper is my therapy,
Nothing else can really do it for
me.

So baby, I've been writing these
poems,
Saying them out loud in hopes
that one day you can also get to
know him.
Him, Jah, Yahweh, Ba Lesa, God,
Love.
The higher Power.
It's giving a bouquet, when all I
needed was a flower.
Living in Abundance and
abundantly living,
My God is so great, that's why
it's worth forgiving.

I've done my part.
My creativity is through him,
Baby, I knew that from the start.
I am, that I am,
Beautiful, wavy, and smart.
Spoken Word Poet,
Bound to creating great art.

Ms Love